Make Your Old Content New Again

SIX STEPS to Getting More Traffic, Money and Followers by Updating Your Existing Posts

KATY WIDRICK

MAKE YOUR OLD CONTENT NEW AGAIN

www.makemediaover.com
katy@makemediaover.com

MAKE YOUR OLD CONTENT NEW AGAIN

CONTENTS

Affiliate Disclosure ix

Introduction Pg 1

1 Step One: Choose the Right Content Pg 7

2 Step Two: Add, Delete, and Update Pg 15

3 Step Three: Republish with a New Date Pg 23

4 Step Four: Remarket Pg 27

5 Step Five: Analyze Pg 31

6 Step Six: Rinse and Repeat Pg 33

Final Words of Wisdom Pg 37

Worksheets and Additional Resources Pg 43

MAKE YOUR OLD CONTENT NEW AGAIN

AFFILIATE DISCLOSURE

The links in this book may be affiliate links. If you click on one of my affiliate links and make a purchase, I may receive a commission for referring you.

Please know that I only recommend resources I believe in and highly recommend.

MAKE YOUR OLD CONTENT NEW AGAIN

x

INTRODUCTION

BEFORE YOU START

One of the things I've always done with my personal blog is use it as a sandbox. It's a place where I can test out new design and development concepts, experiment with social media and content strategies before using them with clients, and where I can try and FAIL at things that seem like good ideas...but aren't.

And that's why I can say for certain that re-optimizing and sometimes even re-publishing old content can make it new again, resulting in more traffic, decreased bounce rates, higher engagement and — ta da! — more impact with less work.

So, let's define what it all means and then we can get down to details.

BUT FIRST — AND I CANNOT STRESS THIS ENOUGH: you need to keep a few things in mind.

- Please back up your site, NOW, before you make any structural changes to your site. If you need a cautionary tale, use mine: "How I Saved Five Websites From a Hacker"). Read the full story at makemediaover.com/hacker.

If you don't back up your site and you break something, you should be able to fix it by accessing your site files by FTP or your cPanel File Manager. But if that sounds stressful now, imagine how you'll feel when you get the white screen of death.

- If you have dates in your permalink structure – as many bloggers do by default – you should not change your publish dates unless and until you decide how you're going to redirect the old structure to the new. It's easier than you might think (see a tutorial from Yoast at makemediaover.com /permalinks and one from WP Explorer at makemediaover.com/permalinks2) but if you don't take the time to consider this, you will break any old bookmarked or shared links, and those 404 errors will have massive SEO consequences. If you don't want to change your permalinks, you can still do a lot of great work on old posts. But don't change the publish date.

- Optimizing the old posts is only half the battle. Once they're updated, you need to routinely and aggressively market these posts on social media, in email newsletters and more.

- Now is the time to be sure that you have Google Analytics installed properly, and that you understand the basics of looking at your traffic sources, top posts and pages and user flow.

Ready to start? Let's go!

KATY WIDRICK

STEP ONE: CHOOSE THE RIGHT CONTENT

Not every post is going to be worth revisiting. So start with a few tasks before ever updating a single word.

Create a list of your most evergreen posts.

These can be tutorials, reviews, recipes, workouts, product roundups, race or event recaps or just about anything else that doesn't feel dated.

For lifecasters, this can be a challenge but it's also a compelling reason to step away from the "here's what I ate, did, wore, etc." posts and really try to make that content as shareable as possible. I tell clients to keep news you can use in mind when building new content.

Create a list of your Top 10 most-read posts from all sources.

With Google Analytics, you can look at Behavior → Site Content → All Pages and see what content has had the most page views and visits, either in the last 30 days or, more helpfully for this exercise, since the beginning of your blog.

Many of my clients are stunned to find out that their most popular posts are items that they had written years earlier and had since forgotten or stopped marketing. If these posts are getting traffic without you trying, imagine what will happen if you put a little effort in? And even scarier...if these posts are old and have bad photos, broken links, outdated information or worse, that's the impression you'll give new visitors about your site overall.

Create a list of your Top 10 landing pages from organic search.

There are a couple of ways to tackle this task.

a) Go to Acquisition→ All Traffic → Source/Medium and then click on google/organic. From there, use the Secondary Dimension drop-down menu to select Behavior → Landing Page.

b) Go to Behavior → Site Content → All Pages. From there, use the Secondary Dimension drop-down menu to select Acquisition → Source. Anything marked Google is search traffic.

<u>Create a list of your Top 10 landing pages from your top social network.</u>

Go to Acquisition → Social → Network Referrals.

You'll see a breakdown of which platforms bring you the most traffic. For each blogger, this will be different! Click on the top platform and you'll see a list of your most popular posts from that traffic source.

Note: If you do prefer using the platform's internal analytics tool, you can usually still export the data.

<u>Create a list of your Top 10 posts with the highest bounce rates.</u>

You can accomplish this by going back to Behavior → Site Content → All Pages and then clicking the bounce rate column to sort from highest to lowest.

Tip: You really only want to look at the posts

that get fairly high traffic, so you can use the Advanced Site Usage filter to only look at posts that have a minimum number of page views. Depending on how much traffic you get per month, you may want to limit it to posts that have at least 100, 1,000, 10,000, etc. page views.

To do that, click the Advanced link to the right of the search box and in the new menu, add a new metric. Select pageviews, greater than and then whatever number makes sense for your site.

Bounce rate is a measure of the people who come to a page or post and then leave without going to a second spot on your site. Personally, I think bounce rate needs more context than a basic analytics report can give. (Learn more at makemediaover.com/ bounce.) But certainly, lower is usually better.

And making it easier and more appealing to click on a second link in a post can have big rewards.

Tip: If you prefer writing all of these down on paper, I've included some worksheets at the back of the book. If you're better with digital records, you can create a spreadsheet and add your own tabs or even export your results from Google Analytics.

KATY WIDRICK

STEP TWO: ADD, DELETE AND UPDATE

Don't worry — it's not as daunting as it may seem.

At this point, you should have about 30-50 posts on your list. (You'll have some duplication when you do the tasks above and it also really depends on how many evergreen posts you've done.) If it's more? Great! Just make sure that you keep track of which ones you've updated. If it's less, that's fine as well. Work on the ones you have and then you can go back and make new lists, this time looking at Top 20, or working on the social platforms you ignored the first time around.

With each post, you want to do at least some of the things on this checklist:

- Make sure there are no typos, broken links or funky formatting.

- Re-shoot or re-¬edit any photographs or graphics that just aren't as good as they could be. I'll admit — I made some doozies when I started blogging, but the beauty of blog posts is that they're not stuck in time. If you're a food blogger, take the time to make the recipe again and get new high resolution photos in beautiful natural light. If you are a parenting blogger and showcase products, consider adding some new shots or even some collages that really highlight the features on each one.

- Add a pinnable graphic so it's easy for people to share your post on Pinterest.

- Add pre-populated Click to Tweet messages so people can one-click share to Twitter.

- Optimize for search engines. I'm a HUGE fan of the Yoast SEO plugin for

Wordpress, which allows you to put in an SEO title, meta description (which appears as the snippet on Google's results pages) and even a featured image for Facebook and Twitter if you want to use something custom for those platforms.

- If you use them, add new affiliate links and/or banner ads. (Why not capitalize on the posts that are already getting a lot of traffic?)

- Check all images for alt tags (and even better, edit the titles and descriptions as well; some Pinterest plugins and tools will pull captions from one of those fields instead).

- Make sure that you've filled out all of

the fields that are visible on your site, particularly the excerpt (often used for content archive pages) and the featured image.

- Customize the sidebar. Depending on how confident you are using widget visibility or even a plugin that allows you to show different content depending on what category or tag a post is in, this can be really useful. (For example, on posts about social media on my site, the sidebar shows other social media links. On posts about fitness, the sidebar shows other fitness links.)

And the big one:

- Add links to relevant content inside

your post that might keep your reader on your site for a second or even third page view.

I find that the best way to do this is to link to categories and/or tags that are dynamic, but you may also want to add links directly to an individual post.

For example, if you're in a post that features a muffin recipe, somewhere in the post, make sure there's a link, a call out box, a graphic or something else that lets readers know that you have an entire category of muffin recipes they can browse. Additionally (or alternatively), link to another popular recipe ("if you like this blueberry bran recipe, you'll love my oatmeal lemon bars — they're delicious and healthy and make for an easy breakfast on the go!").

Or, if the post you're working on gets a lot of traffic from Pinterest, make sure you play to that audience. Link to or even embed relevant pins or boards, and make sure that it's easy for them to follow you on Pinterest. For example, if you're working on a post that includes a treadmill workout, link to and/or embed a board that you've created on Pinterest that has lots of other treadmill workout ideas.

Why do I say do some of these tasks and not all? Because not all of the steps will be relevant to each post. If you have a post that does really well on Pinterest and really doesn't have a great future on Twitter, don't spend too much time optimizing it for Twitter!

But keep in mind: just because you're not active on a particular platform (say, Pinterest) doesn't mean your audience isn't. Even if you don't want to actively market your posts on that social network, you do want to make it as easy for your readers to share to it as possible. So don't discount adding a pinnable image even if Pinterest isn't your jam.

TIP: I really like using Canva because it has the templates already customized to each platform's preferred size and ratio. The free version is great but the premium version (Canva for Work) allows you to save your brand kit, including typography/fonts, colors, etc.

Learn more at makemediaover.com/brand

STEP THREE: REPUBLISH WITH A NEW DATE (OPTIONAL)

I warned you before and I'm doing it again, this time in big scary bold font. That's how important this is.

If you have dates in your permalink

structure — as many bloggers do by default — you should not change your publish dates unless and until you decide how you're going to redirect the old structure to the new. If you don't take the time to consider this, you will break any old bookmarked or shared links, and those 404 errors will have massive SEO consequences. If you don't want to change your permalinks, you can still do a lot of great work on old posts. But don't change the publish date.

What's the benefit to re-publishing? It gets the post back on your home page. It sends it to your RSS subscribers, so they see it in feed readers and email subscriptions. It may get a bigger bump in search engine results because it has a fresher publication date. And it gives you "new" content that you didn't actually have to create from scratch.

But if this freaks you out or just doesn't sit well with you, don't worry! The other steps will have big rewards and this one really isn't required.

MAKE YOUR OLD CONTENT NEW AGAIN

STEP FOUR: REMARKET

Unlike Step Three, which is optional, Step Four is a MUST.

By updating your posts, you may get an organic bump in traffic as search engines see the new and richer data, and visitors click through your new links.

But the key is to share these updated links as much as — no, more — than new posts that you publish.

Here's my typical sharing routine (borrowed heavily from a great workflow that CoSchedule recommends, which you can view at makemediaover.com/workflow):

- Twitter: 3-4 times the first week and then once every other week

- Facebook: once a month

- Pinterest: to a board of my own blog posts immediately and then to as many relevant boards as possible over the next month

- Instagram: immediately upon publishing and then once a month

CoSchedule now has a social templates and automation tool that I find incredibly helpful. You can set up as many templates as you want, with all of the shares set up on a pre-determined calendar and then you just fill in the social messages for each post in one fell swoop! Learn more at makemediaover.com/smtemplates.

> **TIP: I use Tailwind for scheduling my pins and I think it's the best tool because you can pin something to multiple boards at once, but schedule them to go out on any interval you want, so the same pin doesn't go up back-¬to-¬back in your feed.**

I also use two tools for scheduling Instagram: Later.com (makemediaover.com/later) and Grum.co (makemediaover.com/grum), and Iconosquare (makemediaover.com/ iconosquare) for Instagram Analytics.

I keep a very careful eye on my social queue (using CoSchedule; makemediaover.com/ coschedule) so that I never post too much on any given day, and so that I can reschedule items if there's any reason that I no longer want it to go live.

I use this same sharing schedule for new posts, but this ensures that I'm sharing my best content through the week (and it allows me to post a lot less often than I used to, without seeing a decrease in traffic).

STEP FIVE: ANALYZE

My poor clients are probably sick of this phrase, because I'm constantly asking them:

Is it fun? Is it working?

(Learn more at makemediaover/questions)

If it's fun, forget the analytics. That's a pretty awesome metric. If it's working — it's bringing you new page views, more money, more followers or whatever your goal is — keep it up.

And because you're making these changes while creating new content, you'll need to keep looking at your analytics reports to see how successfully your strategy has been. After you do your first few posts, look to see which ones had the biggest growth in traffic, and then use that information wisely. If your tutorial posts start getting a lot of traffic but your product reviews don't, try to figure out why...or let go of the reviews and start creating more tutorials. (Give the people what they want!)

STEP SIX: RINSE AND REPEAT

Once you get through your first list of posts, you may think you're done. You're not. Make sure that as time goes on, you do these same steps for new posts. Don't be afraid to edit an edited post if you want to add newer links or content. Keep that social media queue stocked all the time, and market those popular posts often.

KATY WIDRICK

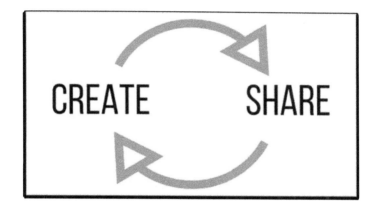

KATY WIDRICK

FINAL WORDS OF WISDOM

You still have to create new content, both for your loyal direct audience and so that Google sees that your site is active. So don't abandon your editorial calendar! If anything, you may want to devote the time you were giving to one weekly post and use that to optimize older content instead.

In some cases, you may decide that some posts not only aren't worth re-optimizing, they're not worth keeping. I recently deleted hundreds of posts on my site that I truly felt were doing me a disservice, because they were so outdated or just totally irrelevant to my current blogging point of view. If you delete posts, you may want to redirect your audience to a new page or post of your site instead, or create a fun 404 page to get people to click something else instead. (Please note: I don't delete any posts that get decent traffic — I only deleted the posts that were rarely viewed and not worth my time to clean up.)

Your site structure is really important, so having dynamic categories or tags that you can link to is really helpful. They're dynamic, which means that every time you add a post to that category or tag, it appears automatically on the page. If you're a food blogger, it's better to link your entire recipe index in a post than an individual recipe, because the recipe index will always have the most recent posts!

Whenever possible, try not to add too much content manually that you could add dynamically. Instead of adding your social links to the bottom of each post, work with your developer or theme to automatically add an author box or social icons in a widget that appears after each entry. (That way, posts that you did back in 2008 will have your Pinterest and Instagram links, even though those platforms didn't exist when you first published!)

And remember that no amount of optimization, pretty graphics, pre-populated Twitter messages or the like is more powerful than great content. Write from your heart.

Share what you know. Try to teach your audience something. And these steps will just enhance how awesome you and your blog already are.

"Either write something worth reading or do something worth writing."

~BENJAMIN FRANKLIN~

MAKE YOUR OLD CONTENT NEW AGAIN

WORKSHEETS & ADDITIONAL RESOURCES

MY TOP TEN LISTS

EVERGREEN POST TITLES

1. _____

2. _____

3. _____

4. _____

5. _____

6. _____

7. _____

8. _____

9. _____

10. _____

NOTES:

OVERALL TITLES

1. _____

2. _____

3. _____

4. _____

5. _____

6. _____

7. _____

8. _____

9. _____

10. _____

NOTES:

SEARCH TITLES

1. _____

2. _____

3. _____

4. _____

5. _____

6. _____

7. _____

8. _____

9. _____

10. _____

NOTES:

SOCIAL POST TITLES

1. _____

2. _____

3. _____

4. _____

5. _____

6. _____

7. _____

8. _____

9. _____

10. _____

NOTES:

BOUNCE RATE TITLES

1. _____

2. _____

3. _____

4. _____

5. _____

6. _____

7. _____

8. _____

9. _____

10. _____

NOTES:

KATY WIDRICK

POST CHECKLIST

☐ FIX TYPOS, BROKEN LINKS, AND FUNKY FORMATTING

☐ EDIT OR ADD NEW PHOTOS AND GRAPHICS

☐ ADD A PINNABLE GRAPHIC

☐ ADD CLICK TO TWEET MESSAGES

☐ OPTIMIZE FOR SEARCH

☐ ADD AFFILIATE LINKS AND/OR BANNER ADS

☐ CHECK IMAGES FOR ALT TAGS

☐ FILL OUT ALL FIELDS

☐ CUSTOMIZE SIDEBAR

MORE RESOURCES

My recommended resources:
makemediaover.com/recommended

10 Ways to Bring New Life to Old Blog Posts:
makemediaover.com/10ways

The Blogging Tactic No One Is Talking About:
Optimizing the Past:
makemediaover.com/past

How to Perform a Content Audit of Your
Blog:
makemediaover.com/contentaudit

How to Correctly Optimize & Structure Blog
Posts for Google:
https://makemediaover.com/structure

CoSchedule Blog:
http://coschedule.com/blog/

I'd love to add you to this list! If you've used
this technique on your blog or website and
want to be featured as a case study, please

email me at katy@makemediaover.com.

MAKE YOUR OLD CONTENT NEW AGAIN

ABOUT THE AUTHOR

Katy Widrick is a personal trainer and group fitness instructor as well as the owner of Make Media Over LLC, a consulting and managed services company for bloggers, online influencers and small business owners. She lives in St. Petersburg, Florida with her husband and two daughters and when she's not training for triathlons, she's probably binge-watching The West Wing or Scandal. Find her at makemediaover.com or on social media @kwidrick.

MAKE YOUR OLD CONTENT NEW AGAIN